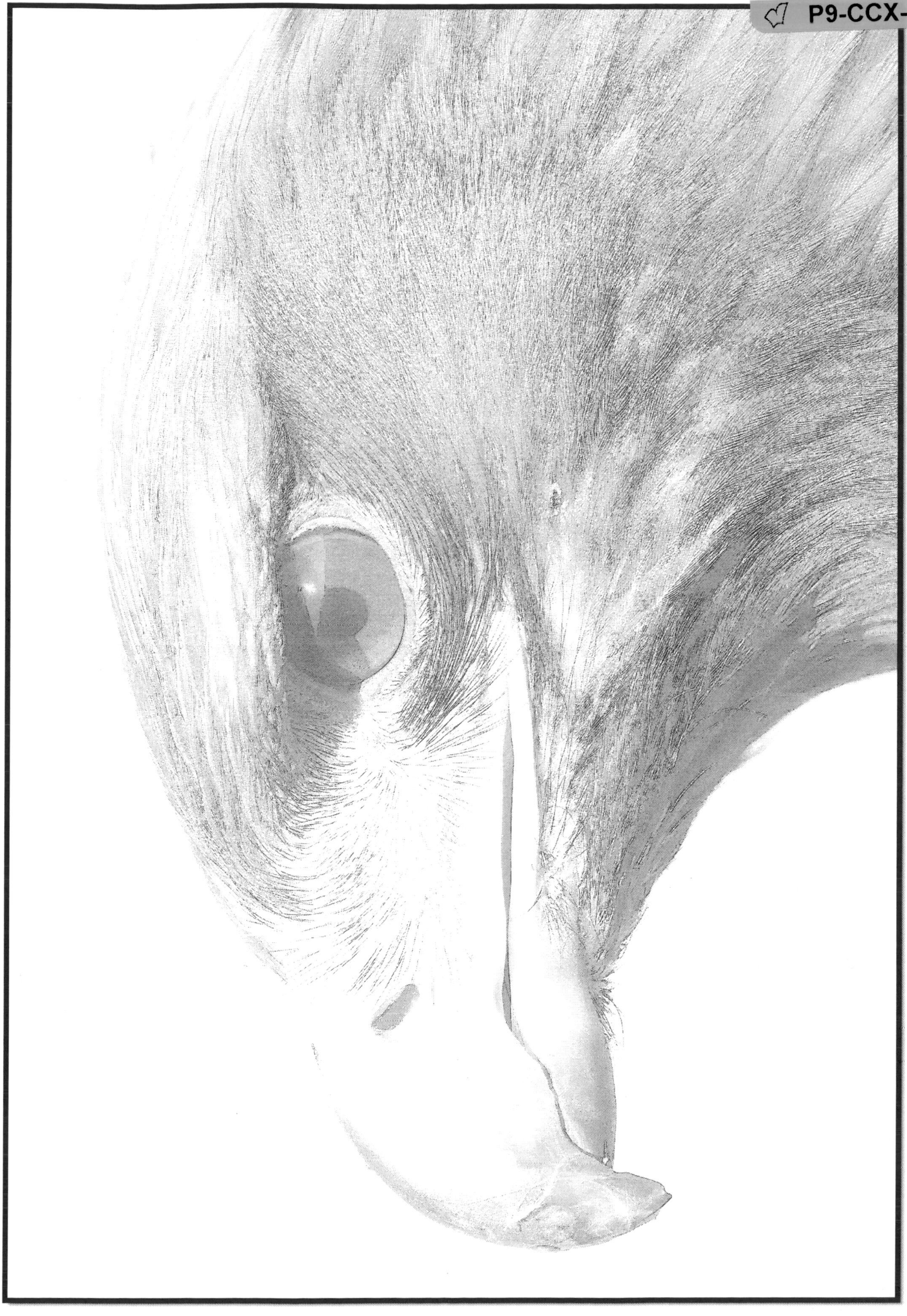

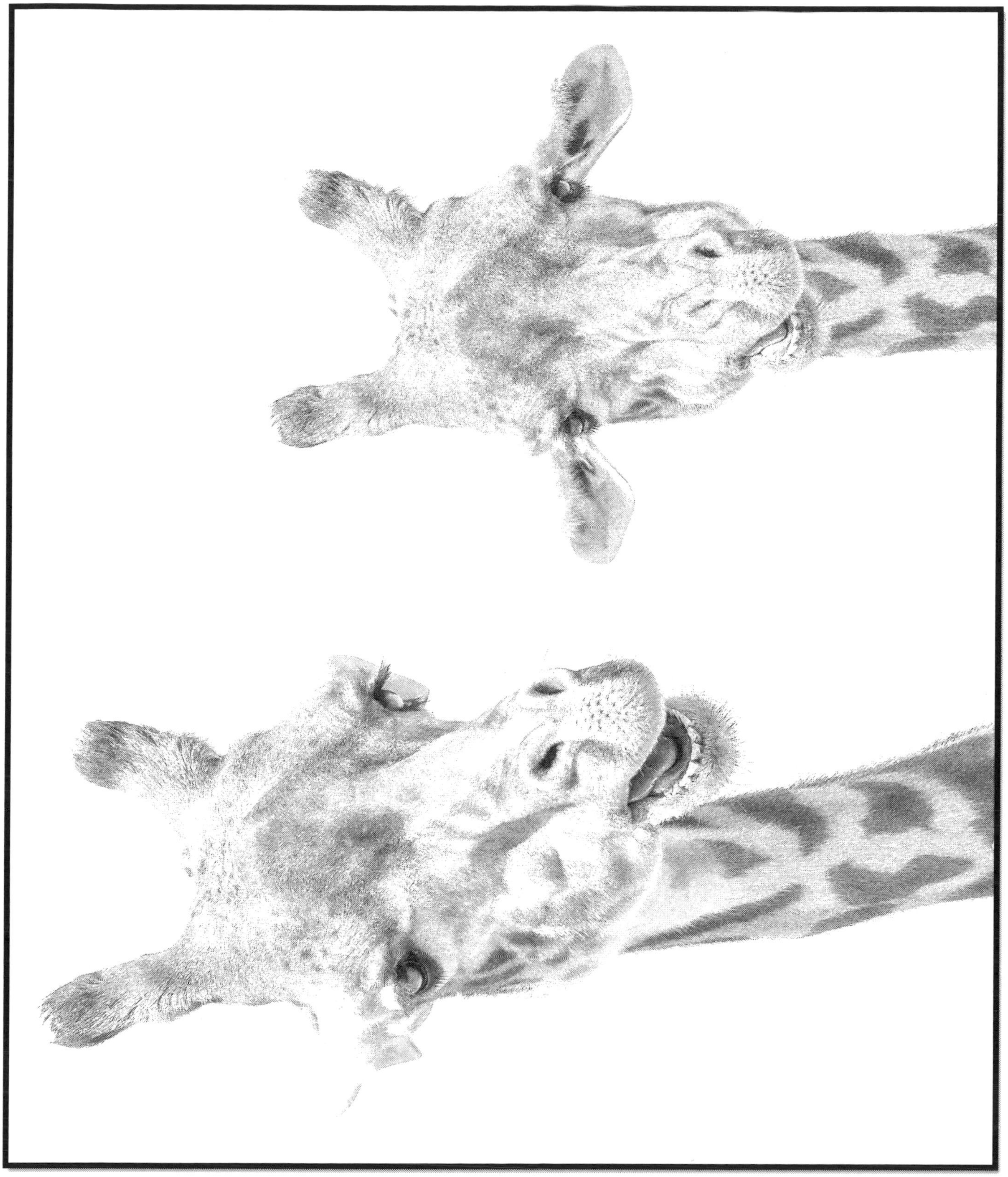

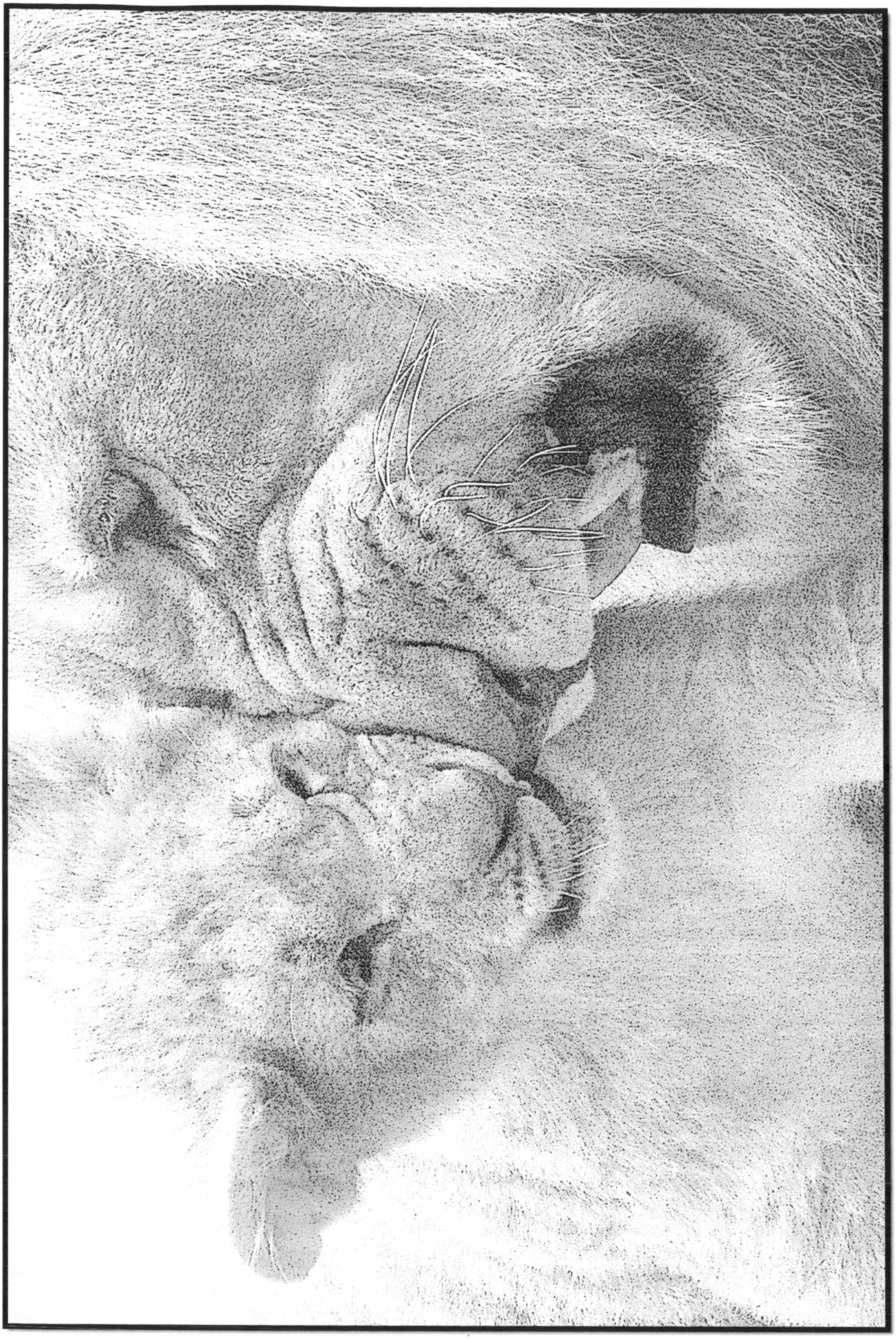

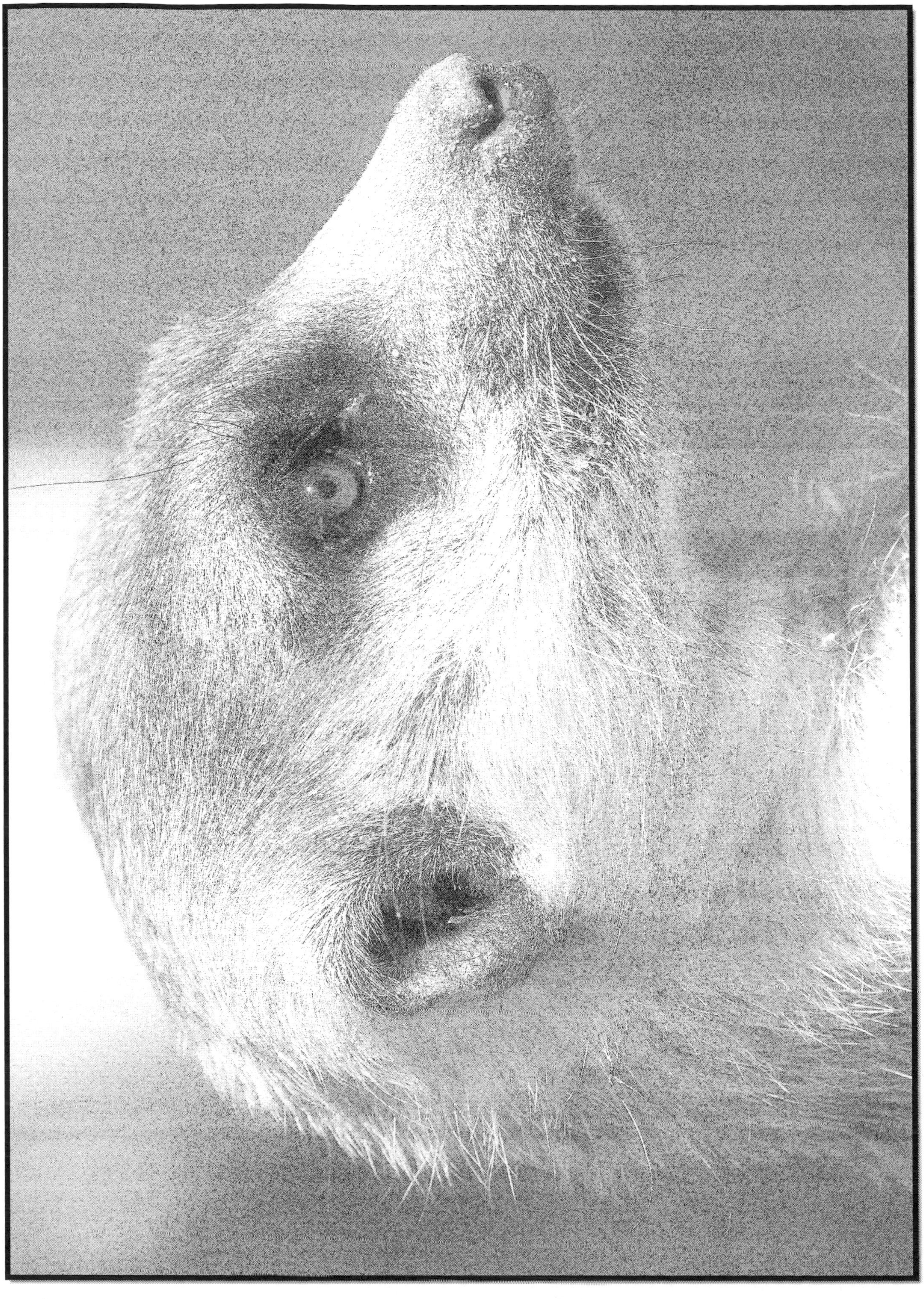

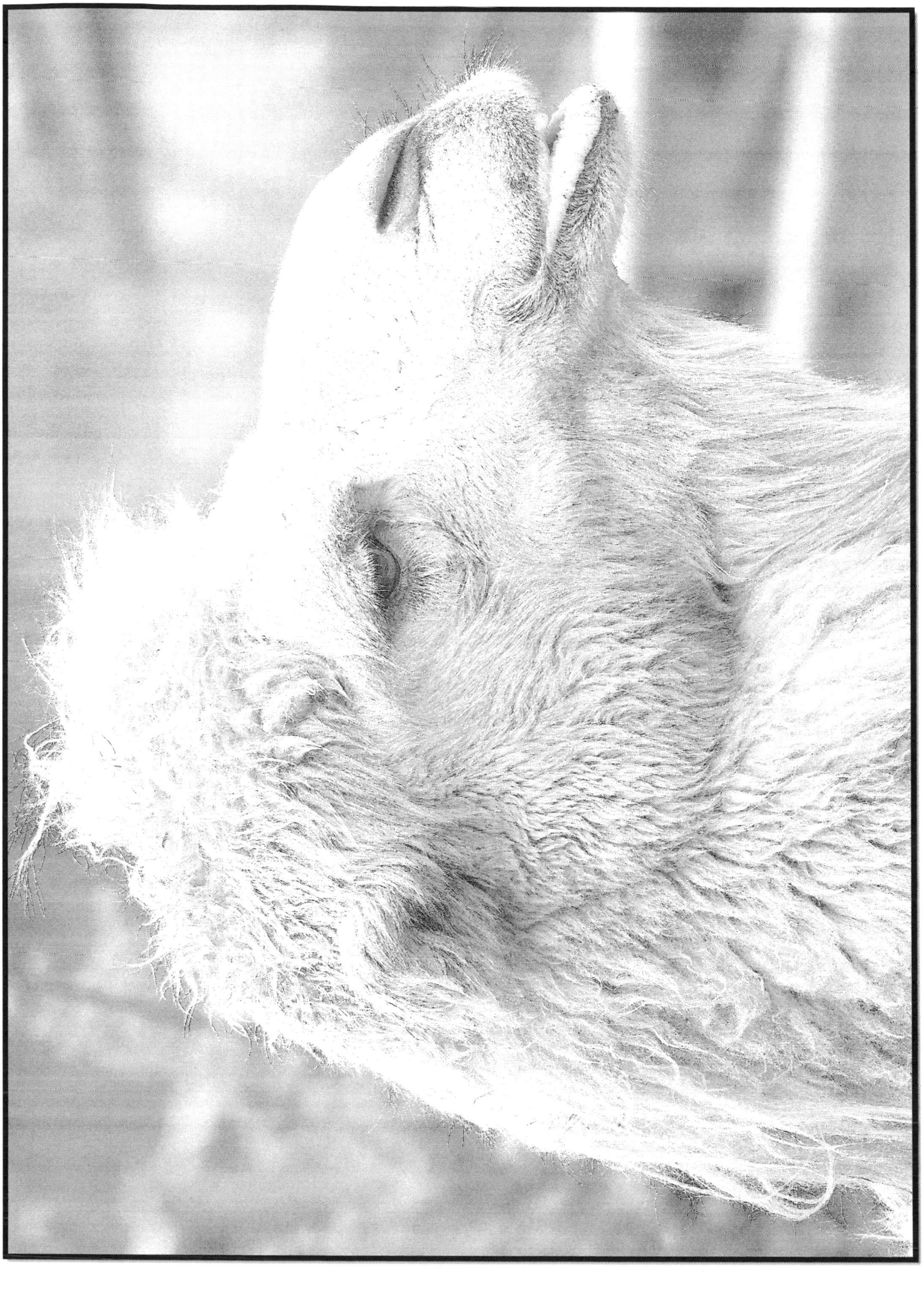

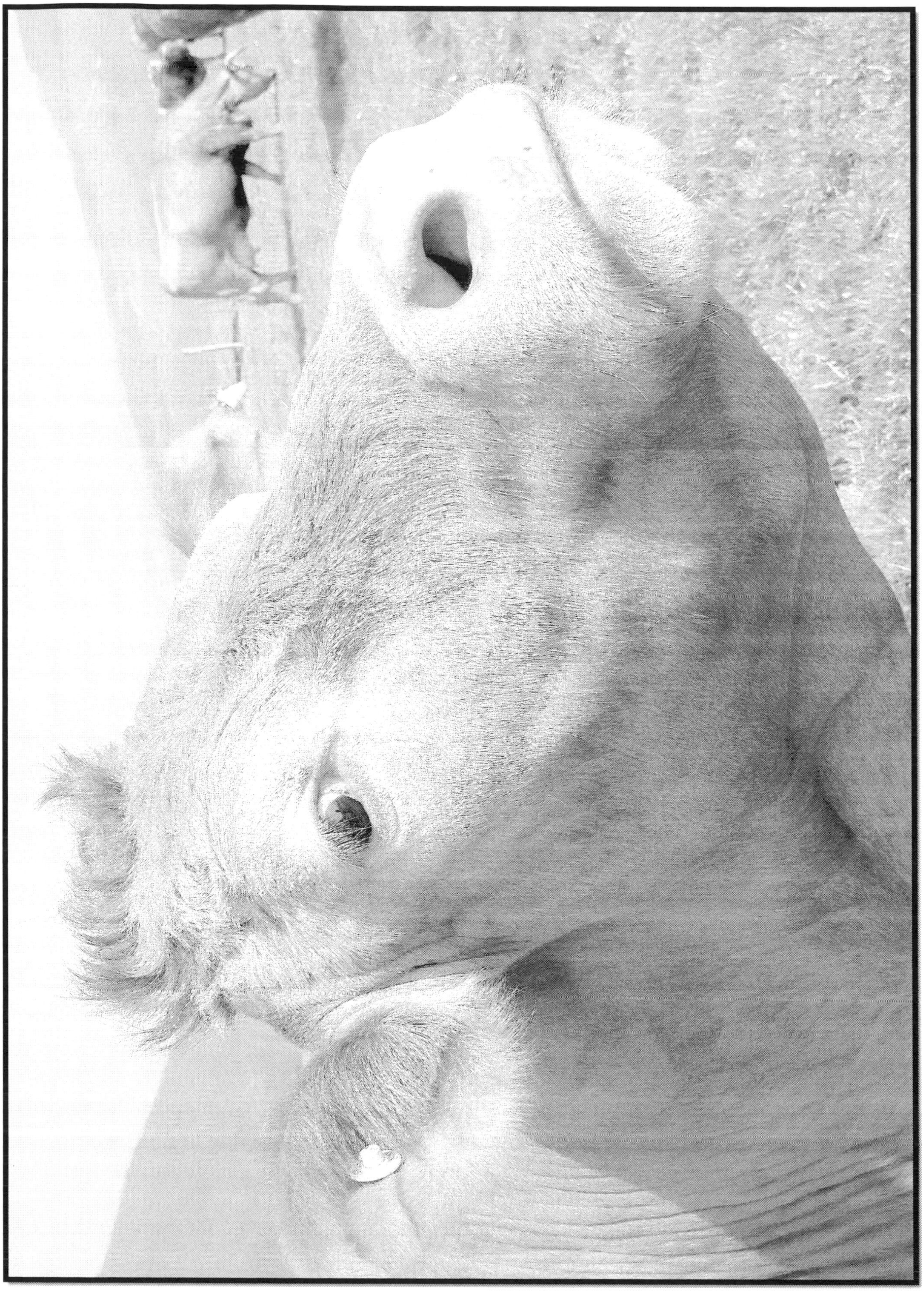

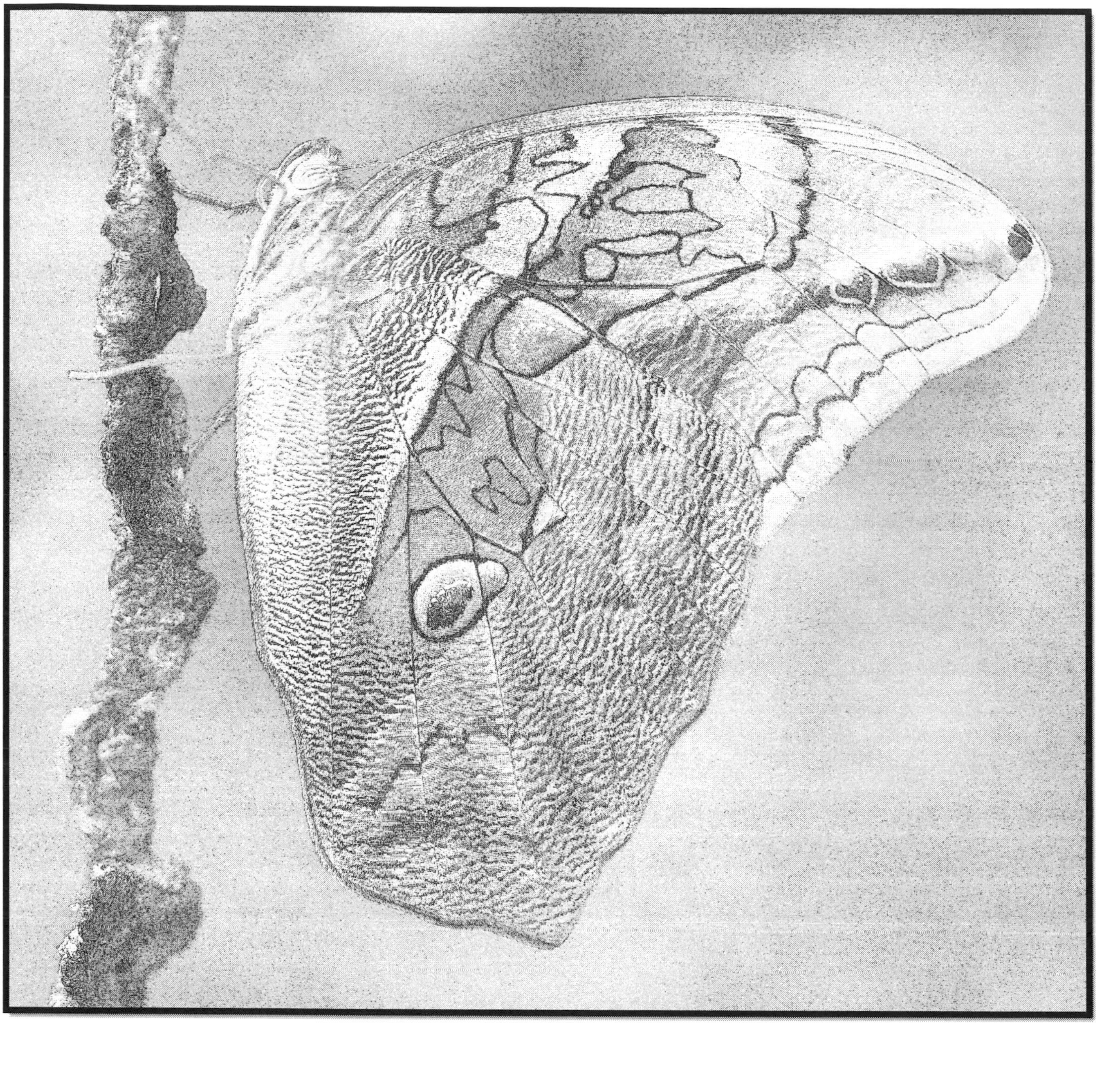

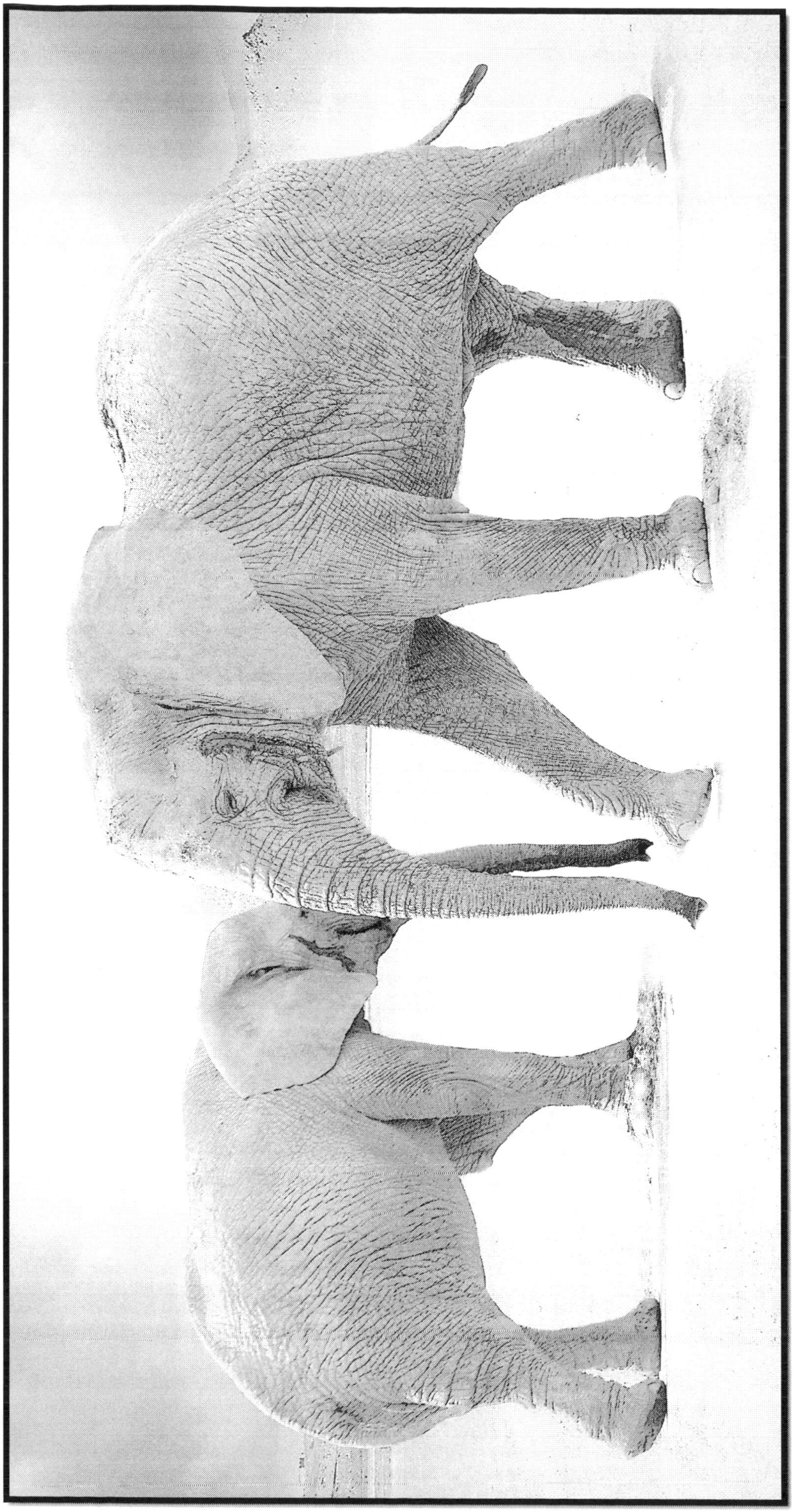

61424701R00057

Made in the USA
Middletown, DE
10 January 2018